OUR BRAINS ARE LIKE COMPUTERS!

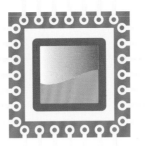

OUR BRAINS ARE LIKE COMPUTERS!

EXPLORING SOCIAL SKILLS AND SOCIAL CAUSE AND EFFECT
WITH CHILDREN ON THE AUTISM SPECTRUM

JOEL SHAUL

Jessica Kingsley *Publishers*
London and Philadelphia

First published in 2016
by Jessica Kingsley Publishers
73 Collier Street
London N1 9BE, UK
and
400 Market Street, Suite 400
Philadelphia, PA 19106, USA

www.jkp.com

Library of Congress Cataloging in Publication Data
A CIP catalog record for this book is available from the Library of Congress

British Library Cataloguing in Publication Data
A CIP catalogue record for this book is available from the British Library

ISBN 978 1 84905 716 5
eISBN 978 1 78450 208 9

Printed and bound in China

CONTENTS

INTRODUCTION

Children with autism spectrum disorders can find other people's thoughts very confusing. Their ability to sort out what other people see, hear, and remember in the social world can be very limited. Many of these children find the order and logic of computers much easier to grasp.

I created *Our Brains Are Like Computers!* to help children whose understanding of computers might exceed their social insight. Computer memory and the internet are employed as metaphors to show how minds take in certain information about other people, store the information, and then pass it on to others. *Our Brains Are Like Computers!* is intended to help children on the autism spectrum to gain a clearer sense of how their own words and behavior can affect other people's minds, so they might "score more likes" in their social world.

Ways to use the book

The book is designed to be read along with a parent, teacher, or therapist, with frequent pauses for discussion. It is important to set a positive tone as you proceed with the book's challenging, weighty material. You should reiterate frequently the essential truth that lots of people have many problems and that admitting to these problems, and working on them, is very good.

One method to encourage such honesty and openness is to employ token rewards. You can photocopy and cut out the play money found on page 80, and give it out liberally when children make insightful comments about themselves. This will help them to think, "I admit to problems – I am good" rather than, "If I admit to problems, that just shows how bad I am."

The Feeling Finder Games (pages 61–63) provide practice in tracing social cause and effect. The first game focuses on how the actions of other people affect the player's own thoughts and emotions. The second game does the opposite, emphasizing the player's own words and actions and how these affect others in both positive and negative ways.

The Other People's "Dislikes" Checklist (pages 78 and 79) has been placed near the end of the book in order to avoid breaking up the book's positive focus. You can go over the checklist with the child at any time. It is helpful to photocopy the checklist and keep it on hand when children are playing the Feeling Finder games and completing the worksheets.

The book contains a number of photocopiable worksheets, each designed to help the child explore how his or her words and actions affect other people. You may find that many children do some of their most thoughtful exploration while completing the worksheets and discussing them with you and with other children. The worksheets vary in their complexity, the amount of writing they require, and whether there is an option to include a drawing on the worksheet as well. It is not necessary for the child to complete every worksheet – a number of worksheets are provided in the book so that you may select the ones that best suit the child's aptitude and preferences.

PART 1

OTHER PEOPLE'S THOUGHTS ARE IMPORTANT

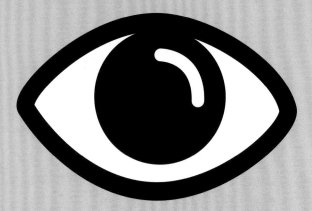

You see other people.

You hear their words.

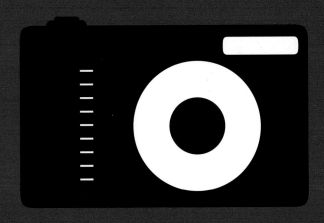

Eyes and ears are like cameras

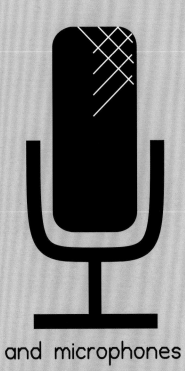

and microphones

to see what people do

and hear what people say.

Other people see *you* and hear *you.*

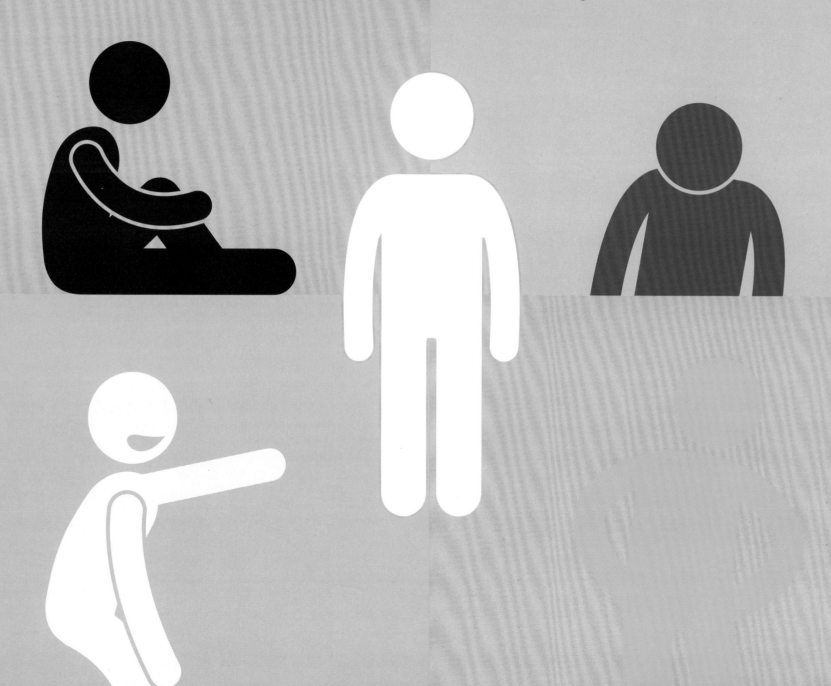

People notice and remember some things about you.

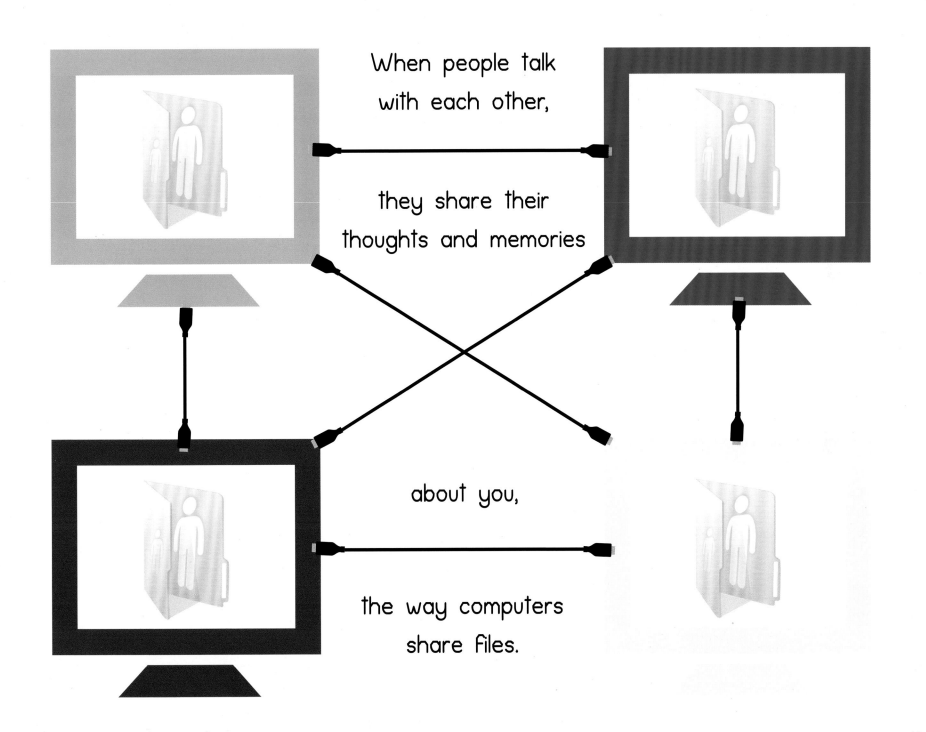

When people talk with each other,

they share their thoughts and memories

about you,

the way computers share files.

It is important to understand other people's thoughts

about *you.*

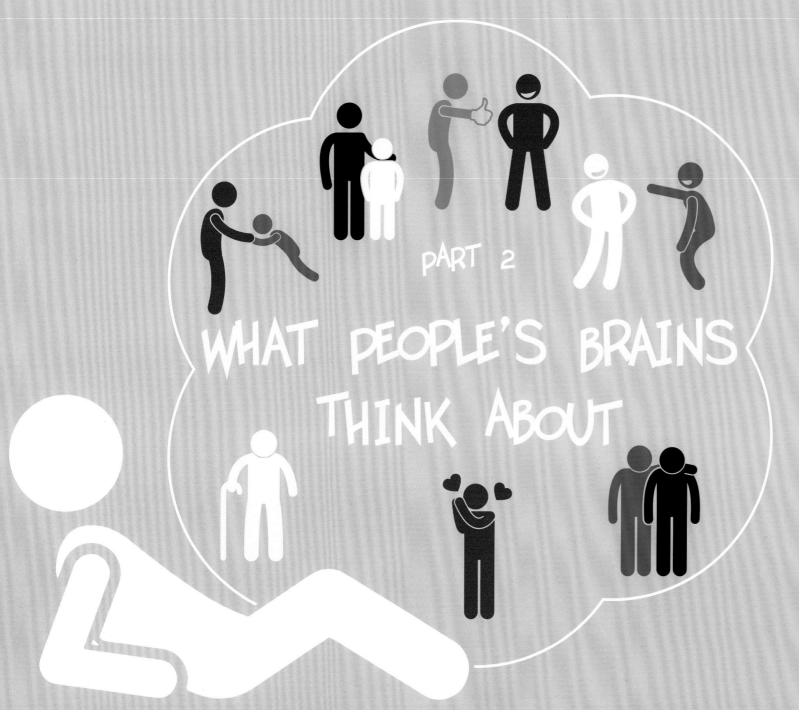

PART 2

WHAT PEOPLE'S BRAINS THINK ABOUT

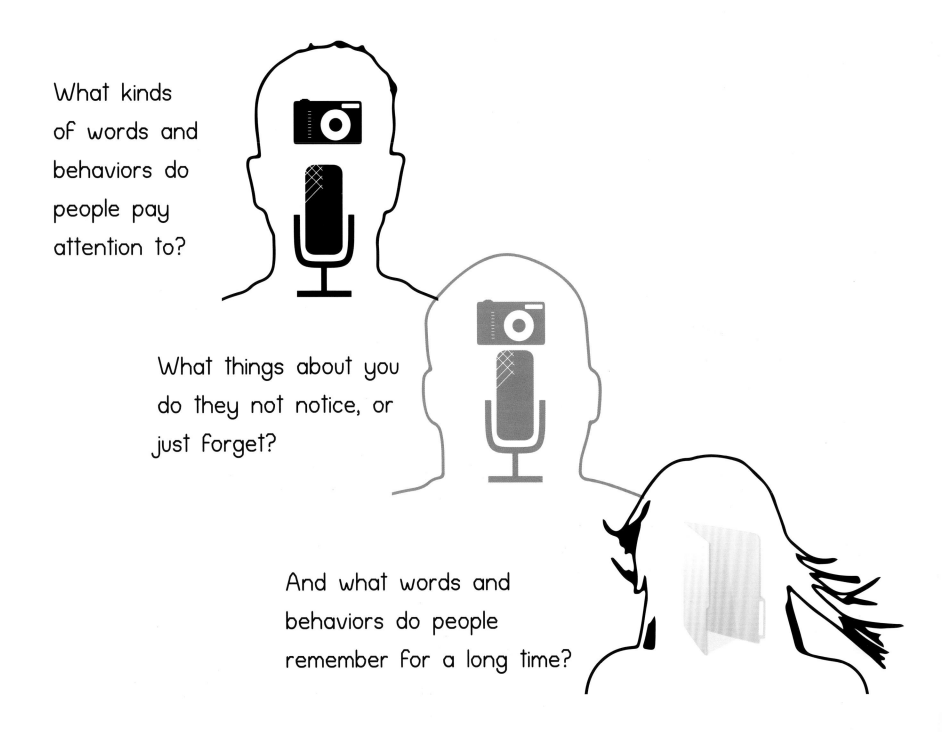

What kinds
of words and
behaviors do
people pay
attention to?

What things about you
do they not notice, or
just forget?

And what words and
behaviors do people
remember for a long time?

People notice and remember things that are *important* to them.

So – just what *is* important to most people?

Look at these five different minds. What kinds of things are on their minds the most?

Most people are thinking about people

much more than they
are thinking about things.

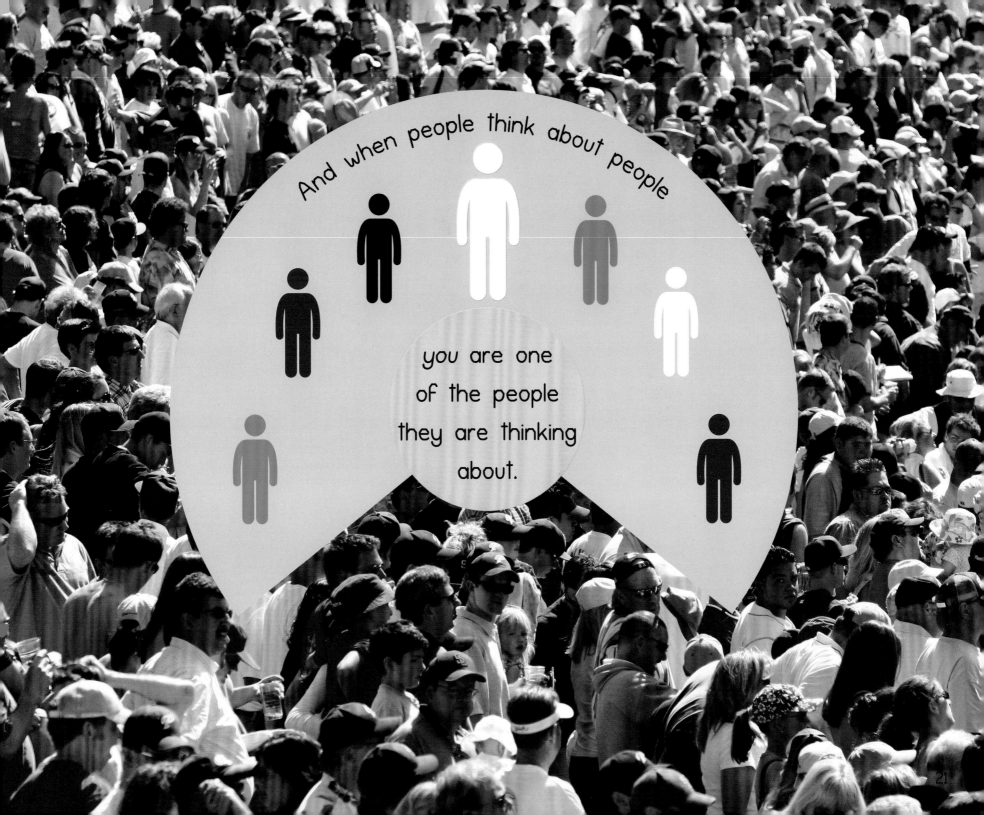

While other people are thinking about you, you should think about them, too.

Even though
it might be
hard at first.

PART 3

WHAT COMPUTERS AND BRAINS REMEMBER

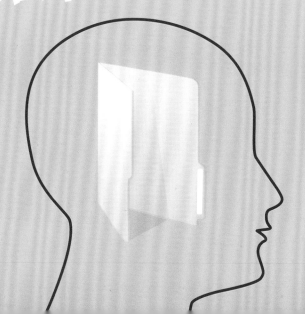

25

Computers remember everything, no matter what, until it is erased.

. . . minutes . . . hours . . . days . . . weeks . . . months . . . years . . .

Brains remember too. But not *everything* in the same way as computers.

Brains let lots of memories go after a while.

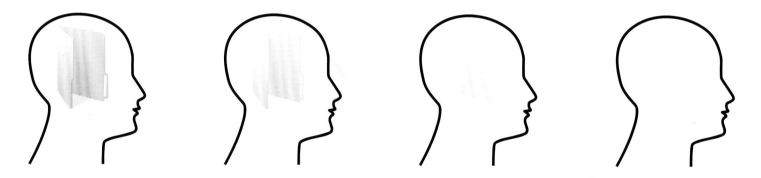

Brains hold on to other "memory files" much stronger and for much longer.

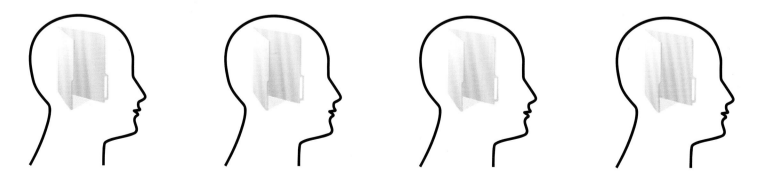

It is important to understand this difference between computers and brains.

In people's minds, memories that are attached to strong feelings often last... and last...and last.

Memories with strong feelings

Memories with strong feelings

Memories with strong feelings

Memories with strong feelings

Memories without strong feelings tend to fade away.

Memories without strong feelings

Memories without strong feelings

Memories without strong feelings

Memories without strong feelings

Let's look at how some memories fade and disappear in people's minds, when the memories don't have strong feelings attached to them.

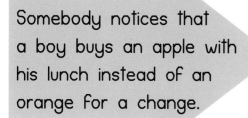
A girl who usually sits in a certain seat in the lunchroom sits somewhere else instead.

Somebody notices that a boy buys an apple with his lunch instead of an orange for a change.

A student asks the person at the next desk, "Hey, have you seen my pencil anywhere?"

But memories with strong feelings are different. Look at these examples of how people create lasting memories by helping other people to have strong, good feelings. These memories fade only a little over time.

. . . minutes . . . hours . . . days . . . weeks . . . months . . . years . . .

Helping someone or caring for them when they really need it.

Paying attention to someone so they really feel noticed and listened to.

Saying, doing, or making something that others find truly interesting.

Saying something kind and encouraging to another person.

You can do this yourself. You can put long-lasting good memories in a person's mind by helping them to have strong, good feelings. Inside the other person's mind, your words and actions might make them feel something like this.

Like they are hearing their favorite music!

Like they are smelling a flower!

Like they are petting a soft kitten!

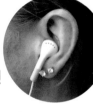

Like they are eating their favorite food!

Like they are getting a present!

Even much later, they may still remember how good you made them feel.

It is also possible to make someone have long-lasting bad memories about you.
There are many ways this can happen – here are just a few.
These memories might fade, but usually they last a long time.

. . . minutes . . . hours . . . days . . . weeks . . . months . . . years . . .

Ignoring someone when they need attention.

Saying mean or rude words.

Unfair or selfish behavior.

Saying or doing something weird or disturbing.

Hurting someone or making them afraid.

31

By giving the other person strong, bad feelings, you can make them feel something like this inside their mind.

Like they are smelling something terrible!

Like their toe is getting stomped on!

Like they are hearing a fire alarm up this close!

Like they are feeling something so cold that it hurts!

Even much later, they may still remember how bad you made them feel.

So, as you go through life you are constantly putting memories into other people's minds – memories about what you do and what you say.

Memories that fade...   Memories that make people feel good...

    Memories that last...   Or that make them feel bad...

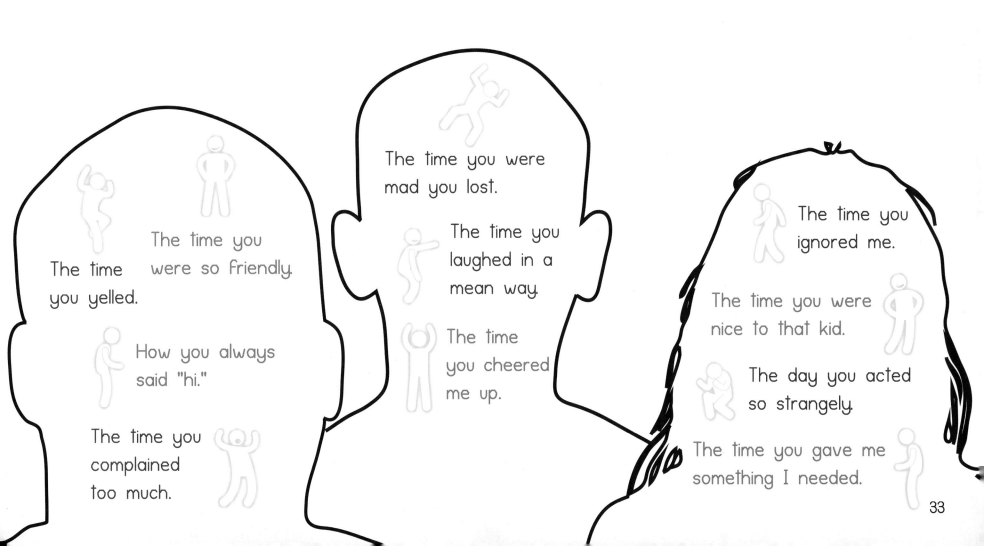

The time you were so friendly.

The time you yelled.

How you always said "hi."

The time you complained too much.

The time you were mad you lost.

The time you laughed in a mean way.

The time you cheered me up.

The time you ignored me.

The time you were nice to that kid.

The day you acted so strangely.

The time you gave me something I needed.

33

Think about it for a while.

What are some long-lasting memories, both good and bad, that you have put into the minds of people you know?

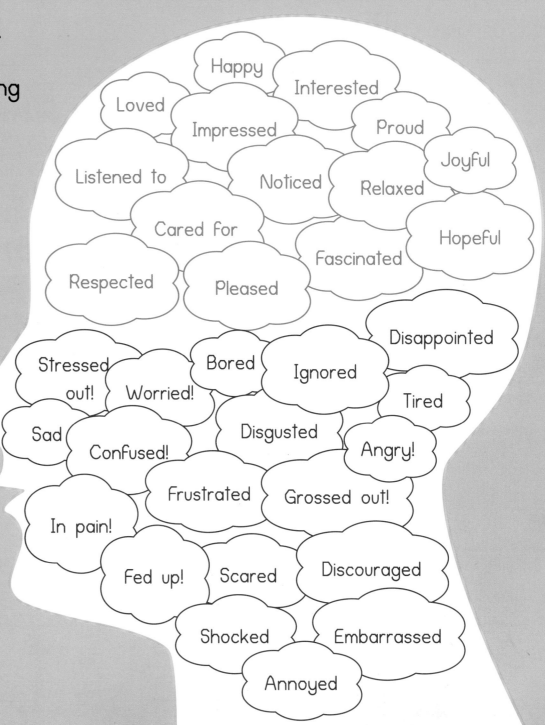

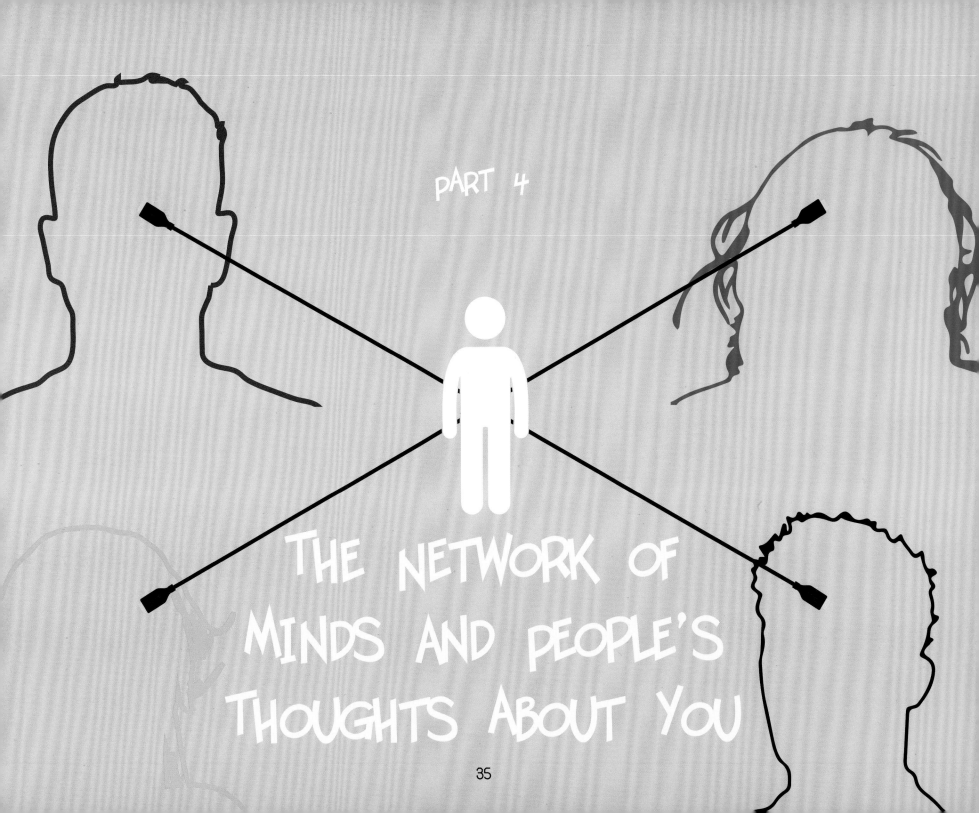

PART 4

THE NETWORK OF
MINDS AND PEOPLE'S
THOUGHTS ABOUT YOU

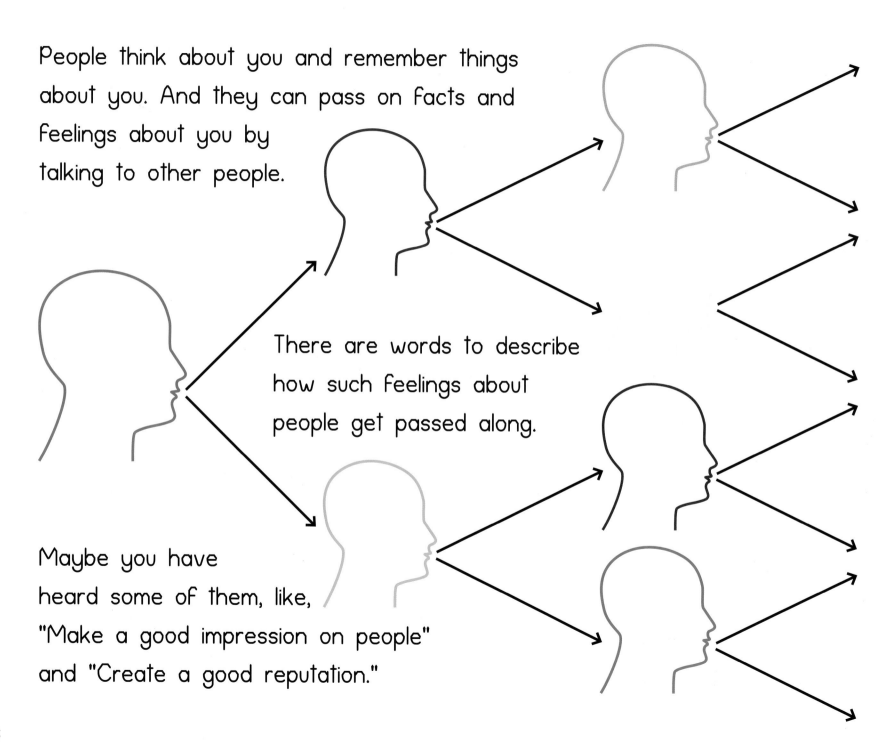

People think about you and remember things about you. And they can pass on facts and feelings about you by talking to other people.

There are words to describe how such feelings about people get passed along.

Maybe you have heard some of them, like, "Make a good impression on people" and "Create a good reputation."

In a way, this is like the internet.

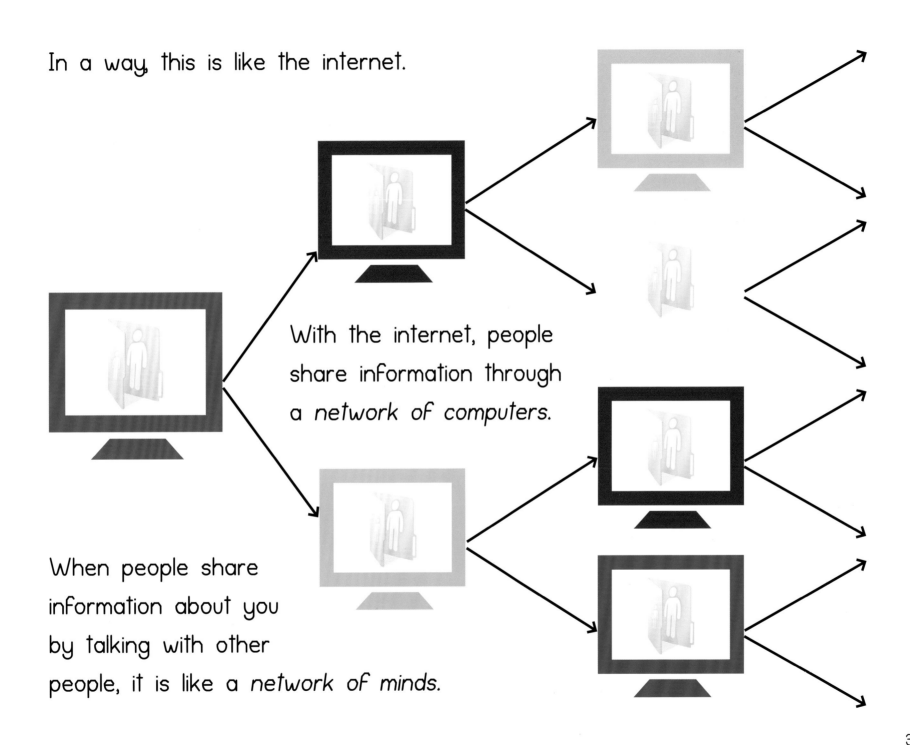

With the internet, people share information through a *network of computers*.

When people share information about you by talking with other people, it is like a *network of minds*.

The network of minds and memories that people like

First, you get "viewed" doing or saying something. For example:

You beat me! You're good at this game!

Way to go!

1

The person either "likes" or "dislikes" what you say or do.

2

The memory about you gets "saved"...

3

...along with all the other memories in this person's mind.

Look! There you are!

4

Way inside the mind, the person makes a decision to "share" feelings and memories about you with someone else.

Hmmm...this is a nice person. I should tell Lisa.

Here's you!

5

This person shares some thoughts and feelings about you with another person.

Hey Lisa... when he lost the game, he was *totally cool* about it!

6

This person decides she "likes" what she has learned about you.

7

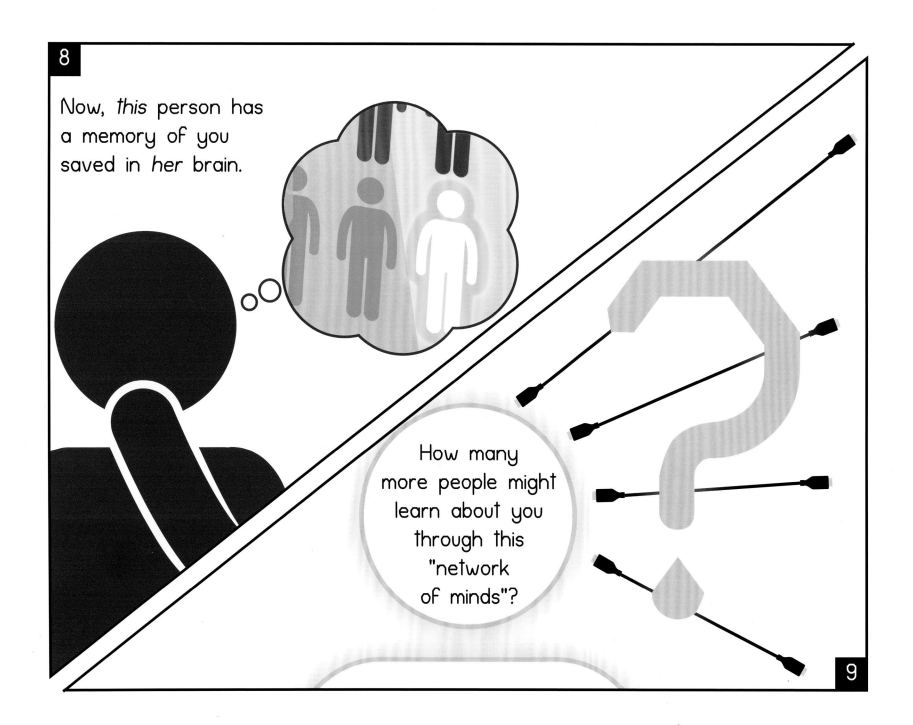

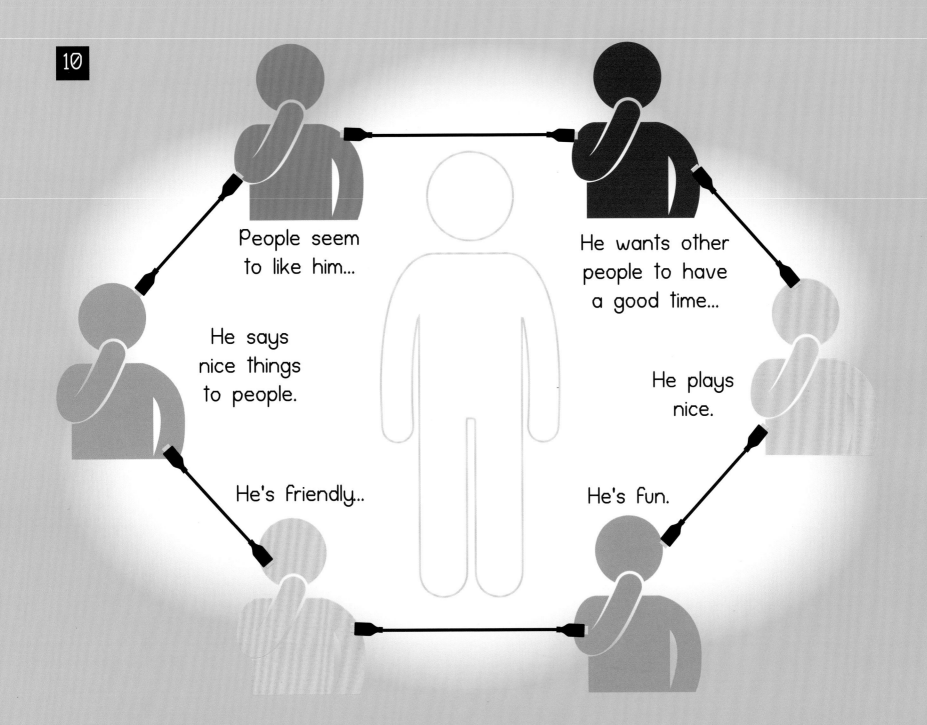

If people like you more than they dislike you, they might be nicer to you.

The network of minds and memories that people don't like

People can also learn and pass on thoughts and memories about you that they do NOT like:

People can save bad memories about you.

Many people might end up remembering things about you that they don't care for.

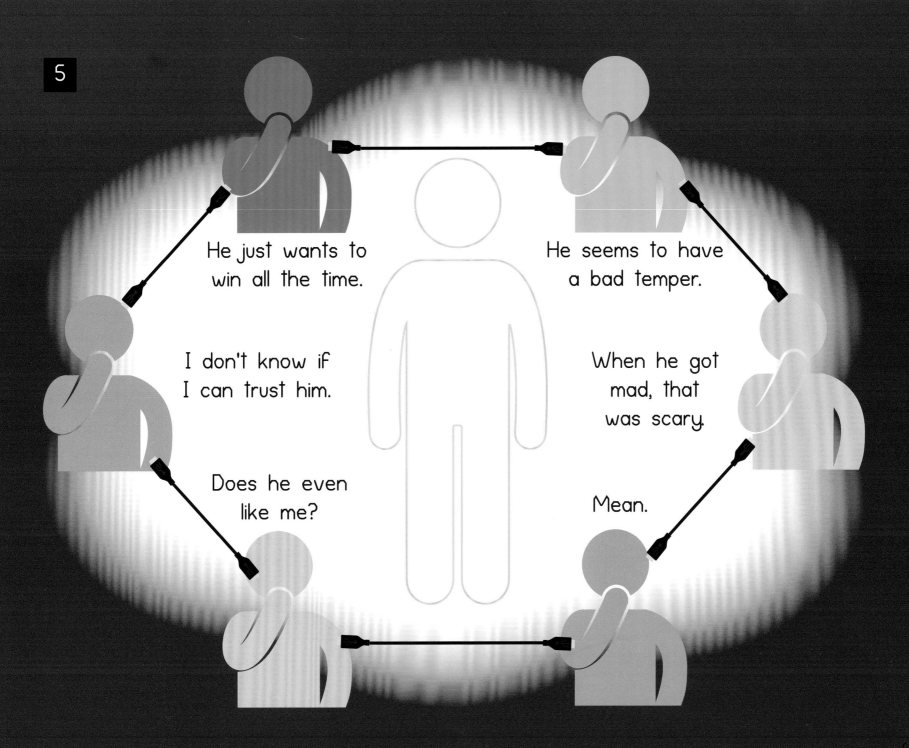

Almost nobody is completely well-liked by everyone.

Usually, it's more like a mixture.

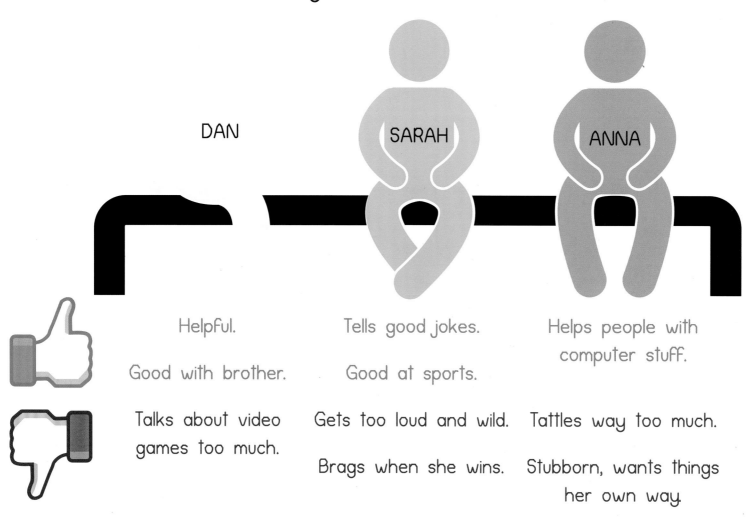

DAN

SARAH

ANNA

Helpful.

Good with brother.

Tells good jokes.

Good at sports.

Helps people with computer stuff.

Talks about video games too much.

Gets too loud and wild.

Brags when she wins.

Tattles way too much.

Stubborn, wants things her own way.

Most people are liked in some ways and kind of disliked in other ways.

Sometimes people dislike a person for bad reasons...even though that person is good, and nice, and interesting.

It is really sad if this happens to you...or to anyone else.

On the next page, look over the examples of good people who are trying hard to get others to understand them and like them. If you know anyone whose good qualities are not appreciated by other people, you should do your part to learn more about these people and to "like" them.

Lots of people say these bad things about Mia:

    She is overweight.

    She has trouble reading.

MIA

But here are some other facts about Mia:

She is never mean to anyone.

She rescued two cats.

She draws cool pictures.

Lots of people say these bad things about Ryan:

    He knows very little about video games.

    He runs really slowly on the playground.

RYAN

But here are some other facts about Ryan:

Ryan was born with problems with his legs. It is still hard to walk.

He tells funny jokes.

He says nice things to people.

PART 5

EXPLORING OTHER PEOPLE'S LIKES AND DISLIKES

Nobody's perfect.

Heard her compliment some girl's make-up.

Complains when work is hard...

Gets mad when she loses video games.

He can be funny sometimes.

He gave me a drink that one time...

Wish he would tie his shoe laces...

Picks his nose...

Brags about his own bike.

Fixed my bike once...

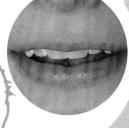

Yes, nobody is perfect...no adult, no kid, not me, and not you.

But we all do some things that other people appreciate...things they might learn about and like.

To help put more good thoughts about you into other people's minds, you must first get a better understanding of what other people really appreciate about you.

Then, you can try hard to do *these* things *more*.

51

Think for a while about the many good things about you. The adult with you will be able to help you think of even more.

Things you know a lot about.

Things you are good at doing.

Good things you have done for others.

Things you have done or said that others have enjoyed.

Hard problems in your life you have worked on.

This next part is harder to think about.

You will need to find out more about things people *don't* care for about you.

Then, you can try hard to do *less of these things* other people *don't* like.

In the pages that follow, you will learn a lot about yourself. And don't worry if you find some problems! Actually, the more problems you admit to, the more you are truly a brave and good person for being willing to explore them.

How to work on your problems

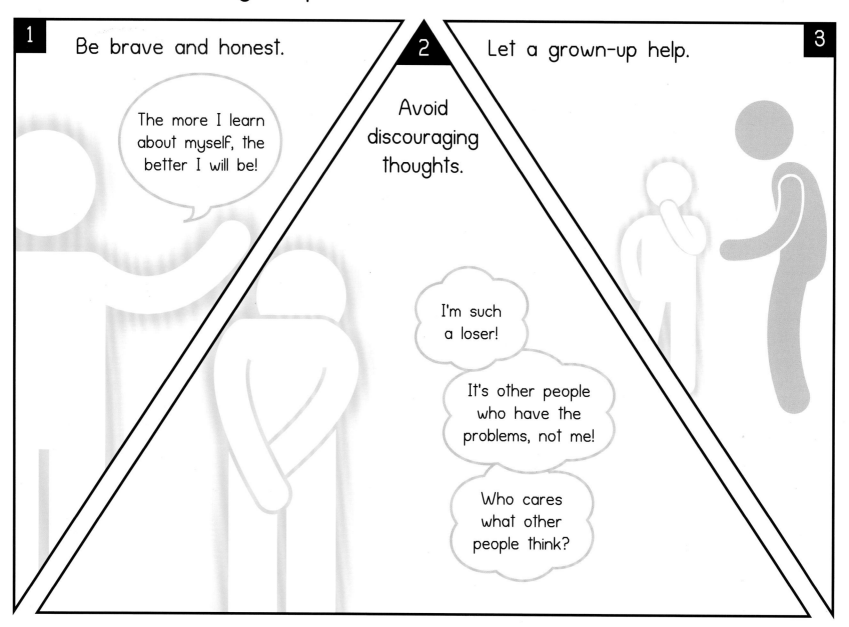

4 Work on what you can change... | instead of what you can't.

People say I should work on my temper. They're probably right.

I can definitely stay clean and dress better. People notice that stuff.

There are a couple of things I do that seem to annoy people. I can work on those things.

I can pay attention to people and show interest in things that seem important to them.

Too much time playing video games keeps me away from people sometimes. I need to be careful with that.

I have only two good friends. I NEED AT LEAST 10!

If I don't play great football, girls will NEVER LIKE ME!

If I can't be a famous video game designer, that will be JUST TERRIBLE!

Some people are mean to me no matter what I do or say. I am HELPLESS in such a mean world.

When I am in noisy, crowded places, I feel just awful! There's NO HOPE for someone like me!

Certain beliefs can slow down your learning about other people's thoughts.

People are just going to think what they want about me, no matter what I do.

I doubt if many people pay much attention to me or remember very much about me.

The things I have done and said in the past are too awful! There is not much I can do now to fix what people think of me.

I am too busy thinking about important stuff to wonder about what other people are thinking.

Use better thoughts and beliefs to stay positive and make progress.

There are few things more important than other people's thoughts and feelings.

People may understand that you had special problems back then, and that you are trying very hard now.

People notice you and pay attention to you more than you realize.

You can't change everyone's mind about you, but some people's thoughts and feelings will change.

Imagine other people's thoughts as you move forward in your life.

Imagine the new and good things
people might find out about you
as you learn and change.

. . . minutes . . . hours . . . days . . . weeks . . . months . . . years . . .

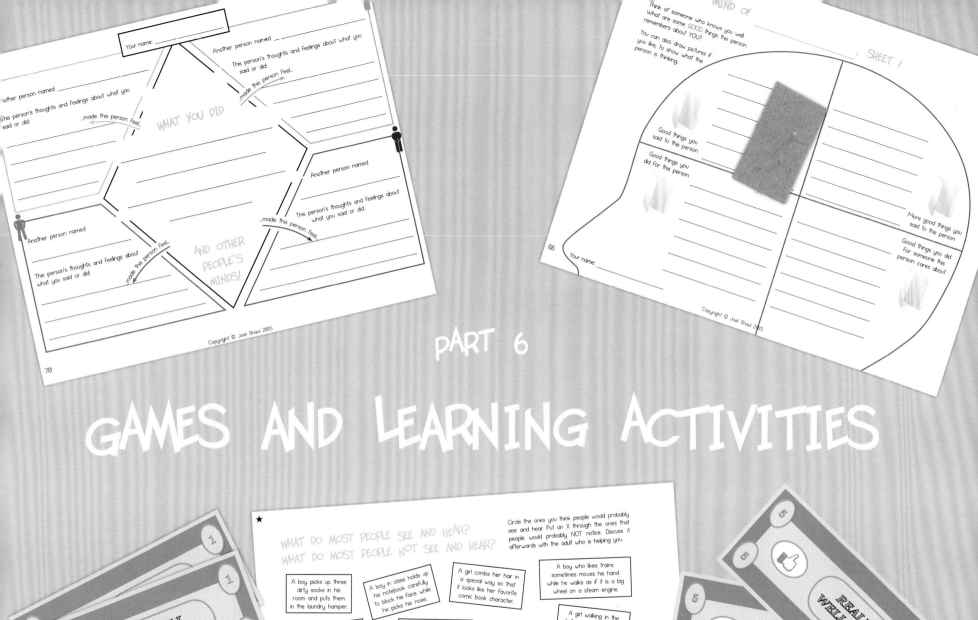

PART 6

GAMES AND LEARNING ACTIVITIES

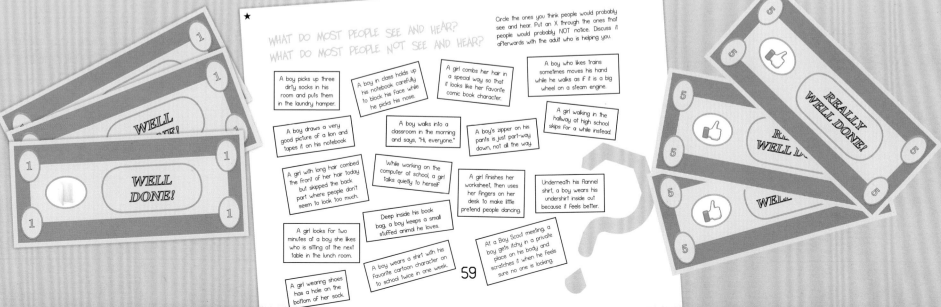

WHAT DO MOST PEOPLE SEE AND HEAR?
WHAT DO MOST PEOPLE NOT SEE AND HEAR?

Circle the ones you think people would probably see and hear. Put an X through the ones that people would probably NOT notice. Discuss it afterwards with the adult who is helping you.

A boy picks up three dirty socks in his room and puts them in the laundry hamper.

A boy in class holds up his notebook carefully to block his face while he picks his nose.

A girl combs her hair in a special way so that it looks like her favorite comic book character.

A boy who likes trains sometimes moves his hand while he walks as if it is a big wheel on a steam engine.

A boy draws a very good picture of a lion and tapes it on his notebook

A boy walks into a classroom in the morning and says, "Hi, everyone."

A boy's zipper on his pants is just part-way down, not all the way

A girl walking in the hallway at high school skips for a while instead.

A girl with long hair combed the front of her hair today but skipped the back part where people don't seem to look too much.

While working on the computer at school, a girl talks quietly to herself

A girl finishes her worksheet, then uses her fingers on her desk to make little pretend people dancing.

Underneath his flannel shirt, a boy wears his undershirt inside out because it feels better.

A girl looks for two minutes at a boy she likes who is sitting at the next table in the lunch room.

Deep inside his book bag, a boy keeps a small stuffed animal he loves.

A girl wearing shoes has a hole on the bottom of her sock.

A boy wears a shirt with his favorite cartoon character on to school twice in one week.

At a Boy Scout meeting, a boy gets itchy in a private place on his body and scratches it when he feels sure no one is looking.

60   Your name: _____

Feeling Finder Game One

1. Open the book at page 62 and place it between you and another player.

2. When it is your turn, flip a coin.

3. If it lands on Heads, answer a Green question.

4. If it lands on Tails, answer a Red question.

You are allowed to ask an adult for clues.

You can play with more than two players.

Feeling Finder Game Two

1. Open the book at page 63 and place it between you and another player.

2. When it is your turn, flip a coin.

3. If it lands on Heads, answer a Green question.

4. If it lands on Tails, answer a Red question.

You are allowed to ask an adult for clues.

You can play with more than two players.

* You can use the Play Money while playing these games.

FEELING FINDER GAME ONE

How other people made you have thoughts and feelings.

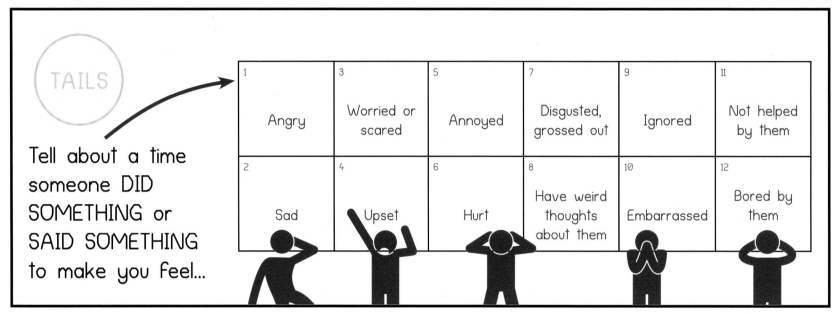

TAILS

Tell about a time someone DID SOMETHING or SAID SOMETHING to make you feel...

1 Angry	3 Worried or scared	5 Annoyed	7 Disgusted, grossed out	9 Ignored	11 Not helped by them
2 Sad	4 Upset	6 Hurt	8 Have weird thoughts about them	10 Embarrassed	12 Bored by them

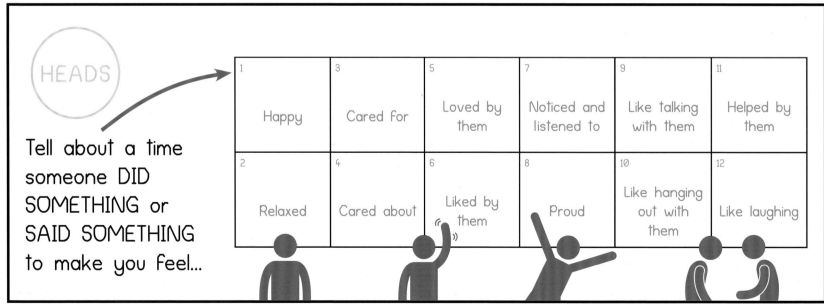

HEADS

Tell about a time someone DID SOMETHING or SAID SOMETHING to make you feel...

1 Happy	3 Cared for	5 Loved by them	7 Noticed and listened to	9 Like talking with them	11 Helped by them
2 Relaxed	4 Cared about	6 Liked by them	8 Proud	10 Like hanging out with them	12 Like laughing

62

FEELING FINDER GAME TWO

How you made other people have thoughts and feelings.

TAILS

Tell about a time you DID SOMETHING or SAID SOMETHING to make someone else feel...

| 1 Angry | 3 Worried or scared | 5 Annoyed | 7 Disgusted, grossed out | 9 Ignored | 11 Not helped by you |
| 2 Sad | 4 Upset | 6 Hurt | 8 Have weird thoughts about you | 10 Embarrassed | 12 Bored by you |

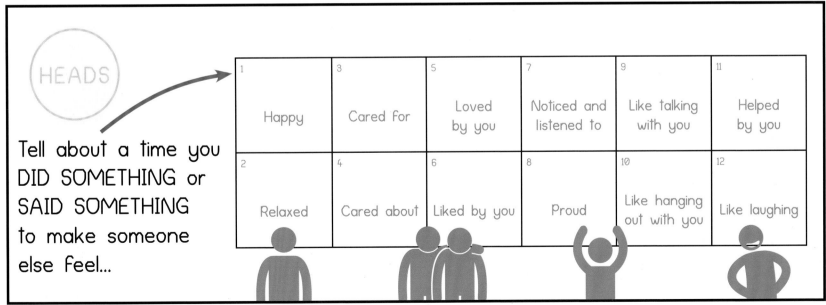

HEADS

Tell about a time you DID SOMETHING or SAID SOMETHING to make someone else feel...

| 1 Happy | 3 Cared for | 5 Loved by you | 7 Noticed and listened to | 9 Like talking with you | 11 Helped by you |
| 2 Relaxed | 4 Cared about | 6 Liked by you | 8 Proud | 10 Like hanging out with you | 12 Like laughing |

63

★

WHEN DID YOU SAY OR DO SOMETHING TO HELP SOMEONE HAVE GOOD FEELINGS?

Think of just one person you know pretty well. What are some things you did that made this person feel good? Fill in the blanks. Draw small pictures too if you like.

I made _____

feel RELAXED when I _____

_____

_____

I made _____

feel PROUD when I _____

_____

_____

This person's name:

_____

I made _____

feel PLEASED when I _____

_____

_____

I made _____

feel HAPPY when I _____

_____

_____

64   Your name: _____

WHEN DID YOU SAY OR DO SOMETHING THAT MIGHT HAVE CAUSED BAD FEELINGS?

Think of just one person you know pretty well. What are some things you did that made this person feel bad? Fill in the blanks. Draw small pictures too if you like.

I made _____

feel ANGRY when I _____

_____

_____

_____

I made _____

feel NERVOUS when I _____

_____

_____

_____

This person's name:

_____

I made _____

feel DISAPPOINTED when I _____

_____

_____

_____

I made _____

feel ASHAMED when I _____

_____

_____

_____

Your name: _____

INSIDE THE MIND OF _____, SHEET 1

Think of someone who knows you well.
What are some GOOD things this person
remembers about YOU?

You can also draw pictures if
you like, to show what the
person is thinking.

Good things you
said to this person

_____

_____

_____

_____

_____

_____

More good things you
said to this person

_____

_____

_____

_____

_____

_____

Good things you
did for this person

_____

_____

_____

_____

Good things you did
for someone this
person cares about

_____

_____

_____

_____

Your name: _____

★

What are some BAD things this person remembers, which the person found difficult about YOU?

You can also draw pictures if you like, to show what the person is thinking.

Time you hurt
this person

Time you used
hurtful words

Time you acted too
weird or immature

Time you made this
person feel tired
or discouraged

_____ _____

_____ _____

_____ _____

_____ _____

_____ _____

_____ _____

_____ _____

_____ _____

_____ _____

_____ _____

_____ _____

_____ _____

_____ _____

_____ _____

Your name: _____

67

★

IMAGINE HOW YOUR WORDS AND ACTIONS CONNECT YOU TO OTHER PEOPLE'S MINDS

Think of something you did or said. Then, imagine how another person felt, and what they said to someone else...

What you did or said:

_____

_____

_____

_____

Then this person had these thoughts and feelings:

_____

_____

_____

_____

Then this person maybe said to someone else about you:

"_____

_____

_____ "

Your name: _____   This person's name: _____

Then this person had these
thoughts and feelings:

_____

_____

_____

_____

Then this person maybe said
to someone else about you:

"_____

_____

_____"

This person's name: _____

This person's name: _____

69

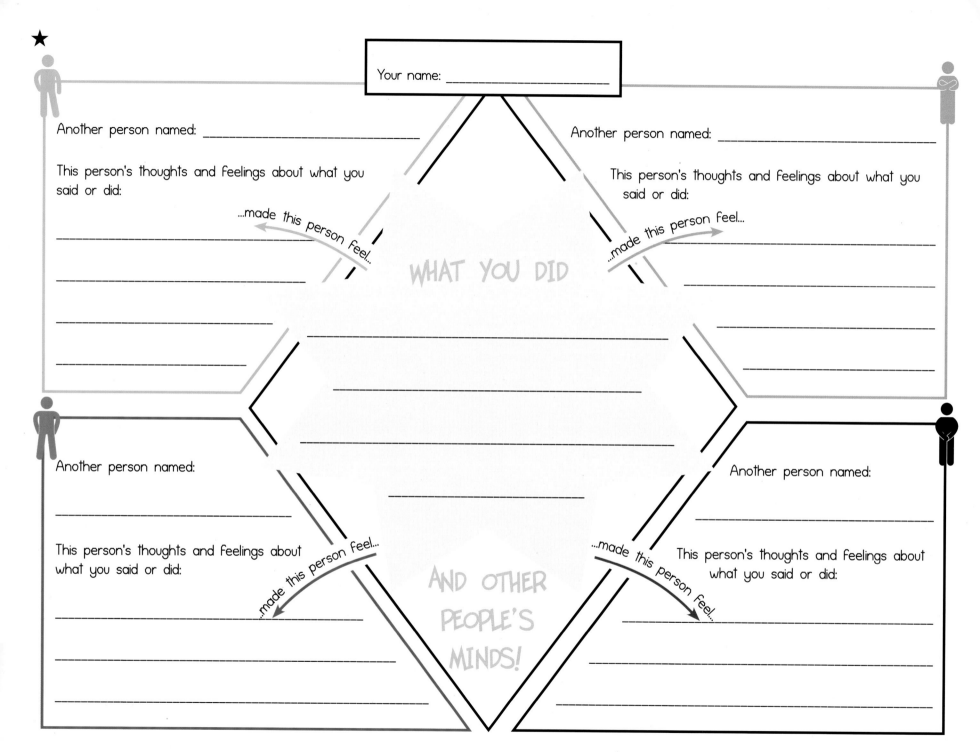

Your name: _____

Another person named: _____

This person's thoughts and feelings about what you said or did:

...made this person feel...

_____

_____

_____

_____

Another person named: _____

This person's thoughts and feelings about what you said or did:

...made this person feel...

_____

_____

_____

_____

WHAT YOU DID

_____

_____

_____

_____

AND OTHER PEOPLE'S MINDS!

Another person named:

_____

This person's thoughts and feelings about what you said or did:

...made this person feel...

_____

_____

_____

Another person named:

_____

This person's thoughts and feelings about what you said or did:

...made this person feel...

_____

_____

_____

70

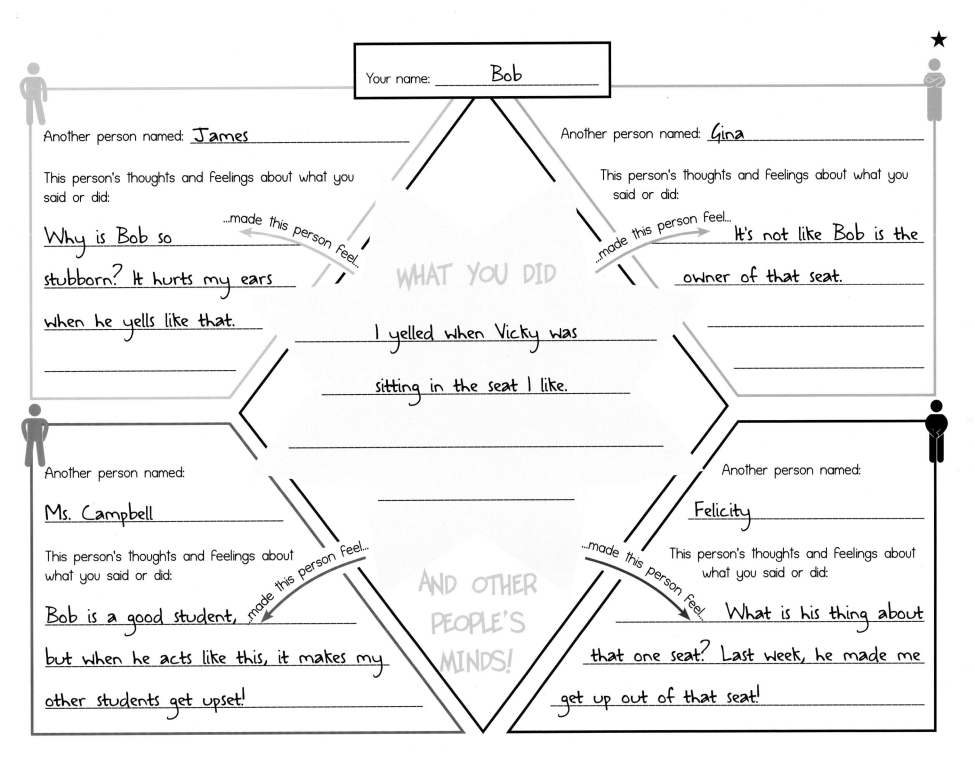

Your name: **Bob**

WHAT YOU DID

I yelled when Vicky was sitting in the seat I like.

AND OTHER PEOPLE'S MINDS!

Another person named: **James**

This person's thoughts and feelings about what you said or did:

...made this person feel...

Why is Bob so stubborn? It hurts my ears when he yells like that.

Another person named: **Gina**

This person's thoughts and feelings about what you said or did:

...made this person feel...

It's not like Bob is the owner of that seat.

Another person named:

Ms. Campbell

This person's thoughts and feelings about what you said or did:

...made this person feel...

Bob is a good student, but when he acts like this, it makes my other students get upset!

Another person named:

Felicity

This person's thoughts and feelings about what you said or did:

...made this person feel...

What is his thing about that one seat? Last week, he made me get up out of that seat!

71

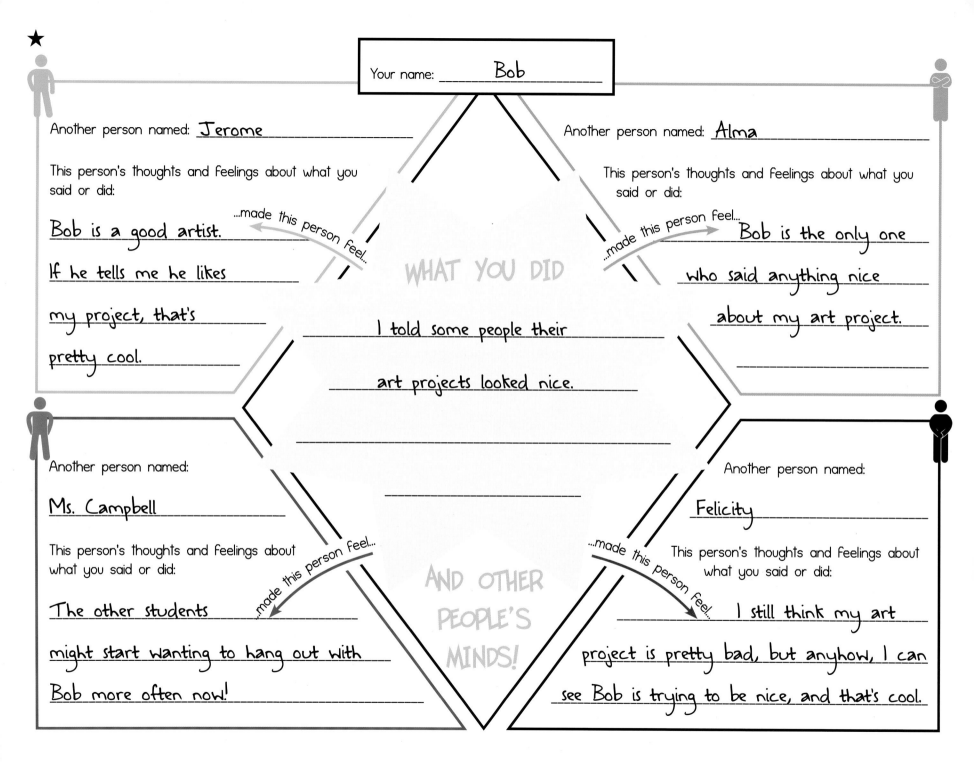

Your name: **Bob**

Another person named: **Jerome**

This person's thoughts and feelings about what you said or did:

Bob is a good artist. If he tells me he likes my project, that's pretty cool.

...made this person feel...

Another person named: **Alma**

This person's thoughts and feelings about what you said or did:

...made this person feel...

Bob is the only one who said anything nice about my art project.

WHAT YOU DID

I told some people their art projects looked nice.

Another person named:

Ms. Campbell

This person's thoughts and feelings about what you said or did:

The other students might start wanting to hang out with Bob more often now!

...made this person feel...

AND OTHER PEOPLE'S MINDS!

...made this person feel...

Another person named:

Felicity

This person's thoughts and feelings about what you said or did:

I still think my art project is pretty bad, but anyhow, I can see Bob is trying to be nice, and that's cool.

72

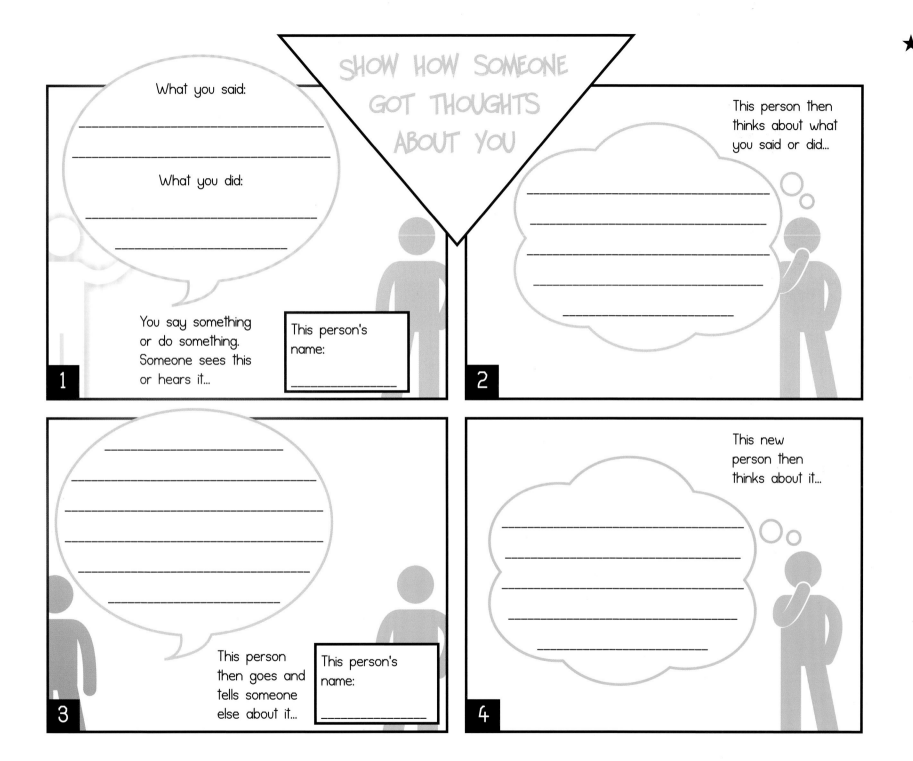

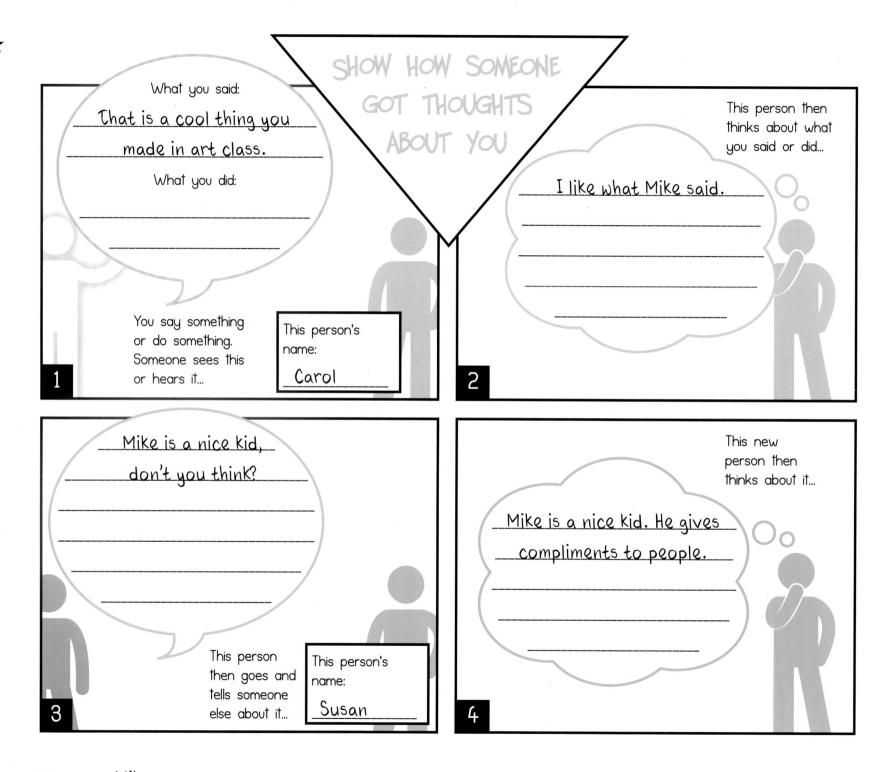

SHOW HOW SOMEONE GOT THOUGHTS ABOUT YOU

1 You say something or do something. Someone sees this or hears it...

What you said:
That is a cool thing you made in art class.

What you did:
_____
_____

This person's name: Carol

2 This person then thinks about what you said or did...

I like what Mike said.
_____
_____
_____
_____

3 This person then goes and tells someone else about it...

Mike is a nice kid, don't you think?
_____
_____
_____

This person's name: Susan

4 This new person then thinks about it...

Mike is a nice kid. He gives compliments to people.
_____
_____
_____

Your name: Mike

NOW, THESE TWO PEOPLE SHARE MEMORIES ABOUT YOU

When they think about you, they have thoughts like this:

"_____
[your name]

is a _____, _____

person."

"_____
[your name]

behaves like this: _____

_____

_____"

When they think about you, they have pictures in their mind like this:

This person's name: _____   Your name: _____   This person's name: _____   75

NOW, THESE TWO PEOPLE SHARE MEMORIES ABOUT YOU

When they think about you, they have thoughts like this:

"_____ Mike _____"
[your name]

is a _____ friendly , nice _____

person."

"_____ Mike _____"
[your name]

behaves like this: He pays attention to

people. When he likes someone he gives

a compliment. _____ "

When they think about you, they have pictures in their mind like this:

This person's name: _____   Your name: _____   This person's name: _____

Other People's Thoughts About You – Past and Future

Write and draw your answers. You are allowed to ask the adult with you for suggestions.

Something you did or said that is a "good" memory for this person:

_____

_____

_____

_____

Something you did or said that is a "bad" memory for this person:

_____

_____

_____

_____

What this person might like about you – things you can do even more:

_____

_____

_____

What this person finds difficult about you – things you can try to do less or stop doing:

_____

_____

_____

This person's name: _____

Your name: _____   77

OTHER PEOPLE'S "DISLIKES" CHECKLIST

No one is perfect! Most of us do some things, or a lot of things, that bother other people. Put a check next to each item that might be something that bothers other people. Feel free to get advice from the adult helping you if you need to.

If you find a lot of problems, don't be upset! You should be pleased that you are good at spotting problems – that in itself is something really great about you.

Talking about something only you want instead of something the other person likes	☐	Paying more attention to online people and things than to real people you know	☐
Not really listening	☐	Not trying to join in when others are playing or hanging out	☐
Getting stuck on your own thoughts instead of the other person's words	☐	Spending too much time doing things you like all by yourself	☐
Not saying hi or goodbye	☐	Getting "lost" in fantasy and pretend in your mind too often	☐
Not using polite words such as please, thanks, excuse me, sorry	☐	"Things" you love becoming more important than people in your life	☐
Talking too loudly or softly	☐	Not trying hard enough with school work	☐
Talking too much or too little	☐	Not doing your share of the work at home	☐
Interrupting	☐	Playing or talking too silly when you should be more calm or serious	☐
Talking out loud to yourself when other people can hear	☐	Playing too wild at times when it annoys people	☐
Getting into "personal space" or touching others when you are not supposed to	☐	Playing or talking too "young" for your age	☐
Not looking towards the person you are talking with	☐	Being bossy or using a "teacher voice" when this is not your job	☐

Paying too much attention to a phone, game, toy etc. when people are around	☐	Tattling on people or correcting them when it is not necessary	☐
Being selfish and expecting more from others than you will do for them	☐	Damaging things because you are angry	☐
Wanting to be first in lines, games, getting a turn, getting called on	☐	Saying you want to hurt someone or break something	☐
Wanting to win too badly; being too disappointed when you lose or don't get your way	☐	Crying or getting too upset when it's not the right time or place to do so	☐
Bragging when you win, or bragging about what you have or what you can do	☐	Picking your nose or doing something else disgusting around other people	☐
Wanting your own way too badly	☐	Sucking your thumb or fingers	☐
Having too many problems with changing plans or routine	☐	Touching private places when others might see this	☐
Bullying or teasing other people	☐	Not keeping your body clean	☐
Not noticing or helping when a person has a problem	☐	Not keeping your hair clean and nice	☐
Not noticing or saying anything when a person is really happy about something	☐	Wearing clothes that are odd, not right for the occasion or not clean and neat	☐
Not asking for help or not accepting help	☐	Leaving your shoes untied	☐
Letting upset feelings make you act mean or scary to others	☐	Moving or behaving in ways that give other people "weird thoughts" about you	☐
Hitting, kicking or shoving others.	☐	Other: _____	☐

79

80